6/93

MUSTANG

POWER-PACKED PONY

BY JAY SCHLEIFER

Crestwood House
New York

Maxwell Macmillan Canada
Toronto

Maxwell Macmillan International
New York   Oxford   Singapore   Sydney

Crestwood House
Macmillan Publishing Company
866 Third Avenue
New York, NY 10022

Maxwell Macmillan Canada, Inc.
1200 Eglinton Avenue East
Suite 200
Don Mills, Ontario M3C 3N1

Macmillan Publishing Company is part of the Maxwell Communication
Group of Companies.

Designed by R Studio T

Printed in the United States of America

10   9   8   7   6   5   4   3   2   1

Library of Congress Cataloging-in-Publication Data
Schleifer, Jay.
Mustang / by Jay Schleifer.—1st ed.
p.   cm.—(Cool classics)
Summary: Describes the design and history of the popular Mustang
car and its effects on popular culture.
ISBN 0-89686-699-8
1. Mustang automobile—Juvenile literature.   [1. Mustang
automobile.]   I. Title.   II. Series.
TL215.M8S35   1992
629.222—dc20   91-27908
                                                   CIP
                                                   AC

CONTENTS

1. Mustang Fever 5

2. Life Before Mustang 6

3. Iacocca's Idea 8

4. That Continental Look! 11

5. Convincing Mr. Ford 15

6. Let's Call It Mustang! 16

7. The Mustang Meets the World 17

8. The Snake Charmer 20

9. Longer, Lower and Heavier 26

10. Here Comes the Boss! 31

11. The Incredible Shrinking Mustang 33

12. Play It Back, Jack! 37

13. SVOs and GTs 42

14. The Future of the Mustang 44

Glossary/Index 47

Meet the horse that made history: the famous Mustang emblem!

1 MUSTANG FEVER

The truck driver carefully steered his 20-ton rig down the street. He was a careful driver. The truck was as big as a house and would do a world of damage if it got out of control.

Then the driver saw a sleek white convertible in a Ford showroom. He'd seen plenty of cars but never one like this. The hood was long and powerful, the back upswept. The driver had read about this new car in the newspapers, and he'd seen it on TV. But here it was in real life. He couldn't take his eyes off it.

While the driver watched the car, the 20-ton truck plowed right through the showroom window.

Luckily nobody was hurt. When the driver crawled from the wreck moments later, his eyes were still glued to the car.

Several states away, another of the pretty white cars arrived at a dealership. It started a riot. People screamed, pushed and waved checkbooks. They all wanted to buy the car.

Not knowing what else to do, the dealer offered it to the highest bidder. He got a fantastic price—and a guest for the night. The winner demanded to sleep in the car so that no one could buy it away from him before his bank opened in the morning.

High above the Atlantic, the man who'd built the white cars was on a business trip to Europe. He was enjoying the fuss his car was causing across America. But he was also glad to be free of it for a few hours.

Suddenly the pilot's voice crackled over a loudspeaker. "Sorry to bother you, Mr. Iacocca, but somebody found out that you're on this flight. Now I've got a ship and two other planes all wanting to talk to you about how they can get a Mustang."

In the spring of 1964 car fever gripped America. It was a wild, young fever. And it had a name: Mustang.

The fever was caused by the new Ford Mustang. There had been many exciting cars before and some since, but nothing has ever rivaled the story of the Mustang.

You're about to read that story.

2 LIFE BEFORE MUSTANG

To understand the story of the Mustang, you need to know what life was like before the Mustang—back in the 1950s.

Walk into a Ford showroom today and say "I want a Ford," and you're likely to get a blank stare from the dealer. Why? Because you didn't say what *kind* of Ford you want. There are at least eight totally different cars all called Ford, from the economic little Escort to the big, brawny Thunderbird.

In the 50s there was basically one Ford. You could get it with a little more decorative trim or a little less. You could have it as a sedan, a hardtop or a station wagon. But it was the same car. "One size fits all."

To carmakers this was a happy world. They only had to create one design. There was only one list of parts to keep in stock. And after the factories were stocked—once each year—all the carmakers had to do was roll them out by the millions, count the cash and smile.

But in the early 1960s there were signs everywhere that the

European sports cars were small and nimble. The Cobra was a combination of an English body and a Ford engine.

buying public was getting a little tired of this arrangement. In California some car owners decided that while one size fit many, it didn't fit them. These people wanted a different look. They painted their cars weird colors, chopped the height of tops, and lowered the bodies until the mufflers nearly dragged on the ground. Taking a brush and a blowtorch to your car was called "customizing." These "Custom Cars" were the wonders of Hollywood Boulevard.

Other drivers simply said no to the big, tail-finned, plushmobiles of the day. Instead they chose cars that were small and nimble. Most were built in Europe. They had names like MG, Triumph and

Porsche. Such cars were called "sports cars."

Most troubling to American carmakers, though, was the mystery of the German-made Volkswagen.

Noisy and cramped, this tiny machine looked like a beetle on wheels. It sat only four people, and had its engine mounted in the rear, where the trunk usually was. Its trunk was up front, where the engine was supposed to be. In an age of powerful V-8s the VW had just a puny 36 horsepower. It was said the only way to lose your license in a VW was to throw it out the window.

Even so, the "Vee-Dub" sold and sold and sold. Nearly half a million of these odd buglike creatures rolled onto American roads each year.

Most American carmakers didn't know what to make of all this. They finally decided that the drivers who bought these little, foreign-made machines were "kooks." There'd always be some around, but they were nothing to worry about.

3 IACOCCA'S IDEA

A few carmakers, though, understood what was really going on. The public was tired of taking whatever Detroit dished out. More and more buyers wanted their cars to fit their needs.

One carmaker who saw this new trend was Lee A. Iacocca. He worked for the giant Ford Motor Company. Lee was one of the smartest people in the car business. Born to an Italian immigrant family, he'd started as a junior **engineer** at Ford in 1946. But he soon discovered he liked selling cars better than designing them. So he moved into the selling end of the business.

What a supersalesman Lee was! Working day and night, he

Lee Iacocca and Henry Ford II

never stopped coming up with new ideas to "move that iron."

When Ford built a dull model in 1956, Lee spruced up sales with a plan that made the car affordable to people with low incomes. The plan was called "56 for '56" and let buyers pay for the car at just $56 a month. It was one of the first easy-payment plans. Sales soared and Lee's idea was copied all across America.

Then Lee got a fateful call from Ford headquarters near Detroit. His success had been noticed. And now, just 36 years old, Lee was named head of the Ford Division. Ford was a giant company that

The two-seat Thunderbird was Ford's answer to the
European cars.

was broken down into several divisions. And the Ford Division was
the most important part of the company. This son of poor
immigrants would make billion-dollar decisions about the cars
that would be sold under the Ford name.

Iacocca surrounded himself with other bright young car guys.
They went to dinner together once a week at a local hotel. At these
dinners they talked about building cars to fit the needs of special
groups of people.

One group was young buyers. There were millions of them! They were into sports, good looks and fun. They liked excitement in their lives—and in their cars, but American carmakers weren't giving it to them . . . yet. That was why many had turned to customizing their cars, or buying cars from other countries.

Lee and his fellow Ford workers made an important decision. They'd create a new car for fun-loving young buyers.

 **THAT CONTINENTAL LOOK!**

At first this car existed only in the minds of its builders. It had no shape and was known as the "T-5" and other code names.

But it did have a description: The car would be small, light and quick. It would look like a sports car and seem to be moving even when it was standing still. Most important, the price would be low enough that young people could afford to buy one. If someone had more money, extras could be added.

Iacocca knew that it would cost over $300 million to build this car from scratch. As rich as Ford was, the company would never risk that much to try his new idea. Not long before the company had tried building a new family sedan called the Edsel and they'd failed miserably. A quarter of a billion dollars had been lost! The company was in no mood to repeat that mistake.

But Lee came up with a way to cut down the risk. Among Ford's plain jane sedans was a car called the Falcon. It had a good engine and lots of well-designed parts, but its glory was hidden under looks that gave new meaning to the word dull. If Lee added a sharp-looking body to the Falcon parts, it would really cut the cost of his new car. The parts weren't special, but it was better than no car at all. The "T-5" now became the "Special Falcon."

Mustang design featured jet air scoops on each side and full round wheel openings for a high-performance look.

Iacocca had to decide how many people the car would seat. Sports cars usually seated only two, and did not sell well. Most car buyers wanted more than two seats. So the new car would seat four. This way, young families would buy it. But, the team members wondered, could a four seater be made to look young and sporty?

It was vital that the new car look good. Without great looks, Iacocca's dream machine would be just another car. With this in mind the **designers** set to work. They produced more than 18 different full-sized **clay models** over the course of a year. Some were nice looking, but not one was just right.

By now it was mid-1962 and Iacocca had a major problem. To get the most attention for his new car, he had planned to unveil it at the 1964 New York World's Fair, an event the whole world would watch. This meant that he had only two years to design and build his car. This usually took twice as long. And the days were flying by. Iacocca needed a final design for the car—fast!

To help the designers understand what he wanted, Iacocca told them about how he'd joined Ford in the first place. While still in college, Lee was visited by a Ford manager looking for bright young people to join the firm. The man had arrived in a Lincoln Continental, the company's fanciest model at the time.

Lee had fallen in love with the Continental. It had a long hood and short rear, giving the car a look of great power and grace. Now Lee suggested that his designers try the same look in designs for the new sportster.

Iacocca also suggested something else: a contest. This would help Ford get a good design in the shortest time possible. All the company's designers took part—whether they worked on Fords, Lincolns and Mercurys, or even trucks. Lee wanted every ounce of talent that Ford had on the project. The contestants were given just two weeks to create a full-sized clay model. This kind of model usually took months to make, but it was now or never.

The designers took the challenge and ran with it. They worked days, nights and weekends. And just 14 days later, seven models gleamed in the sunny courtyard of Ford headquarters. Top managers walked around and around them, viewing them from all sides. The anxious creators watched.

Several of the designs were exciting, but one seemed to catch everyone's eye. It was a sharp, white two-door designed by a group led by two of Ford's top designers, Joe Oros and L. David Ash. They called their car "Cougar."

Unlike the typical fat, finned car of the times, the Cougar was lean and mean. In front it featured a high, narrow grille like the air scoop on a jet. The sides were clean and free of shiny chrome. The tail swept up and ended in three taillights on each side. The roof had a square shape, like an expensive limousine, yet it looked sporty. In fact, the roof design was a lot like the Lincoln Continental. Everyone agreed that the Cougar was the clear winner.

Everyone who was there, that is. Lee still had to convince the rest of the company to build the new sporty car. And at Ford Motor Company, convincing the company often meant convincing one man: Henry Ford II.

First called "T-5," then "Special Falcon" and then "Cougar," this is the look America would soon call the Mustang.

5 CONVINCING MR. FORD

"H.F. II," as he was called, was the grandson of the company's founder, the original Henry Ford. He was no pushover. Rich and powerful, his word was law at Ford. If anyone argued with Mr. Ford, he'd tell them, "Go look at whose name is on the building." At that point the argument ended.

Carefully Lee prepared to show the new car to the big boss. Numbers and facts were gathered. Plans were written out in great detail. The model was cleaned up and perfected. Finally the great day came.

As Ford listened, Lee talked on and on in his best supersalesman style. He counted how many young people were in the market, and explained how they wanted something different from the current models. He proudly proved how little his new car would cost to build because it used Falcon parts. He pointed out that . . .

Suddenly, in midsentence, Henry got up. "I'm leaving," he bellowed. Then he turned his back on Lee and walked out the door.

Lee was crushed. "I got shot down on my favorite project today," he later told his wife.

As it turned out, Henry's leaving had nothing to do with the car. He'd become ill and went straight to the hospital. He spent the next six weeks in bed!

When Mr. Ford returned, Lee presented the car again. This time the boss didn't turn down Lee's car. But he didn't approve it either. He had other things on his mind.

Lee needed a way to get the boss to pay attention to the car, and he needed one quickly! He found a way. Iacocca leaked news about the car to newspaper reporters and car magazine writers. Every time Henry Ford was interviewed, someone asked him when the new car would come out.

Finally Henry had had enough. He called Lee in. "I'm sick of hearing about that car of yours," he told Lee, who by now had just about given up on his dream machine. "If we build it can you sell it?"

"Yes!" Lee shouted.

"Well," Henry shouted right back, "you darn well better, because I'm going to approve it!"

 **6 LET'S CALL IT MUSTANG!**

With the okay to go into production, there were final decisions to be made. One was the name.

The designers had called the car "Cougar" but Lee favored something European—perhaps because the model had been inspired by European sports cars. The team talked about it and finally decided to call the car "Turino" after the city in Italy. Nameplates were designed and photos were taken. The new "Ford Turino" would soon be produced.

At the last minute Lee got a call. Henry Ford had started going out with an Italian woman and Ford executives were afraid that giving the new car an Italian name would cause gossip. "You'll have to pick another name," Lee was told.

With time running short, a Ford man rushed to the Detroit Public Library to search for names that would work. Ford had had luck with animal names like Thunderbird and Falcon. So the man headed straight for the "zoo" books. He came back with a long list

of wild beasts.

His top choices included Puma, Cheetah and Colt. But there was another...Mustang.

Mustang! It was a wild horse that lived in the mountains of the West. Suddenly the Ford men knew they had it! "It sounded like wide open spaces and was as American as could be," Iacocca remembers. What better name could there be for this new animal from the land of the red, white, and blue! "Let's call it Mustang," Lee told the group.

Iacocca sent final orders to his factories. The Ford Mustang would be shown for the first time at the New York World's Fair on April 17, 1964.

7 THE MUSTANG MEETS THE WORLD

Introducing a new car is as much show business as it is business. And Lee Iacocca is a master showman. His goal was to get everyone in America talking about the car.

Advertising was one way to do this. Ford bought ads for the Mustang in more than 2,600 newspapers and magazines. But Lee also wanted the car written up in the news.

In some cases news stories were easy to get. Editors of college newspapers were invited to Detroit to preview the car. That got word to the young people Lee had targeted as future buyers. Then 100 reporters from big city papers were given Mustangs and sent off on a drive across America. Their papers wrote about the car, and so did papers in many towns that the parade passed through.

It was harder to get into major magazines like *Time* and *Newsweek*. Their pages were usually reserved for news about world leaders and great events, not new cars.

But the Ford men knew just what to do—use the desire every reporter has to get the first scoop on a hot story.

"You really should put the Mustang on your cover," a Ford man told an editor at *Newsweek*.

"No chance," the editor replied. "It's just a car. But I admit it's a nice car. I might even buy one."

"Oh," said the Ford man. "Then you'll be the *second* person in New York to have a Mustang."

"Who was the first?"

"Oh, just some fellow over at *Time*."

When *Time* and *Newsweek* came out, the Mustang was on *both* their covers—an incredible victory. "That alone was good for 100,000 sales," Iacocca said later.

The car was officially put on sale on April 17, 1964, at a price of just $2,368. It was about the same price as the usual Detroit sedan. But it was a car with sports-car looks and driving fun.

Within days America had caught Mustang fever. Four *million* people rushed to Ford dealers the first week, causing riots. Crowds were so thick that mechanics in one city didn't have time enough to get the cars off the wash racks and put them into the showroom. In some places police had to be called out to keep order.

Mustang ads described the excitement the car could bring to buyers' lives. In one ad a shy-looking fellow suddenly turns into a swinging playboy. "Wow! What happened to Henry?" people ask. "A Mustang happened to Henry!" a pretty girl replies, as she drives off with him in the car.

Whatever "Henry" wanted in a car, he could get in a Mustang. There was a long list of extras that let a driver customize his or her Mustang into anything from a luxury model to a road rocket. Owners could choose a thrifty V-6 or a hot V-8, a stick shift or an automatic. Extra gauges and electric windows could be ordered.

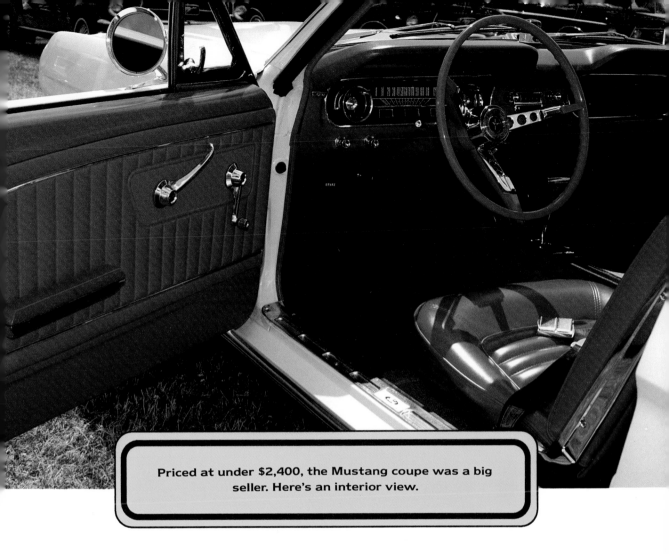

Priced at under $2,400, the Mustang coupe was a big
seller. Here's an interior view.

These items were not usually found on inexpensive cars. The typical Mustang owner paid a low $2,400 for the car, then added a thousand dollars in extras!

What's more, the two-door car came in two models: a hardtop and a convertible. A streamlined **fastback** model was added later. And you could get your 'Stang in wonderful colors. One shade was palomino gold.

The car was especially popular with women. One rock band put out a song about a female Mustang owner. The song, "Mustang Sally," made the hit parade.

Car magazines tested the Mustang and fell in love with it. Although many parts came from the lowly Falcon, nobody seemed to mind. One writer even came up with a new name for low-priced, easy-to-own sporty cars. He called these machines "ponycars," a name that's been around ever since.

Needless to say, sales skyrocketed. Lee had guessed he might sell 100,000 Mustangs in a year. He sold that many in four months! Two Ford factories had been building Mustangs. Now Lee added a third. He was betting billions of dollars that his success would continue.

Iacocca won his bet. The previous best-selling Ford had been the Falcon, selling just over 417,000 cars in its first year. Iacocca set out to beat that record by the Mustang's first birthday, April 17. The man who invented "56 for '56" now came up with the slogan, "417 by 4/17." On April 17, 1965, a red convertible was sold in California, breaking the record with room to spare. More than 418,000 Mustangs were sold in the car's first year. And more than 550,000 were sold in the Mustang's second year. This meant that nearly a *million* Mustangs were roaming the roads within two years! The American car business had never seen anything like it!

A sign in a restaurant put it best: "Our hotcakes are selling like Mustangs!"

8 THE SNAKE CHARMER

The first Mustang was a sporty car, not a sports car. It was built from economy car parts and had no chance of beating real high-performance machines like the Jaguar or Chevrolet's new Corvette Sting Ray. Yet Iacocca knew sales would soar even higher if a real racing Mustang could be built. He also knew just the magician to turn that trick…a slow talkin', fast-drivin' Texan named Caroll Shelby.

Shelby, an ex-race-car driver, had strong connections to Ford. A few years before, he'd created a hot new sports car by stuffing a Ford V-8 engine into a lightweight, English-built two-seat sports-car body. The car he made was the famous Cobra.

One day Shelby was called to Lee's office. When he heard what Iacocca wanted, he probably thought that building a race car from Falcon parts was impossible! But in time he saw how he could do it.

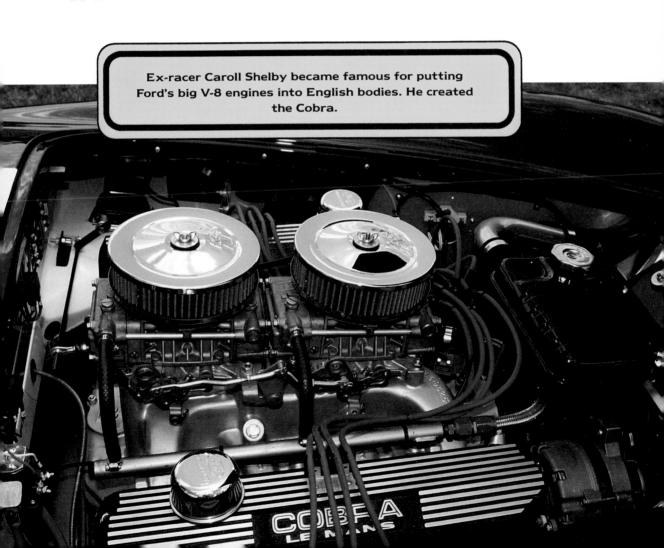

Ex-racer Caroll Shelby became famous for putting Ford's big V-8 engines into English bodies. He created the Cobra.

The Mustang already had the wonderful Ford 289-cubic-inch V-8, the same engine Shelby had used in the Cobra. The car was also fairly lightweight. He'd just have to hot-rod the engine, lighten the body, and put in stronger parts to handle the increased power. Compared to a Jaguar or 'Vette the car would be crude, like a homebuilt hot rod. But it would move!

Before long, 100 half-built Mustang fastbacks with V-8 engines, all painted white, were delivered to Shelby's shop. His men tore into them. The 289 V-8 was pumped to 306 horsepower. The suspension was strengthened. The backseats came out. And the body got a pair of wide, blue racing stripes. When the job was done, Shelby had built the most rip-roaring, hard-riding Mustang ever. Now he had to name it.

Several meetings were held with the Ford men, but nobody could agree on what to call the beast. Finally Shelby got tired of all the nonsense. "I just asked how far it was to the building across the street," Caroll told reporters later. "Somebody checked and said '350 feet.' So we just named the car the G.T. 350."

There was one more step to take before the car could be raced. Racing rules stated that 100 copies of the car had to be built by a certain date. This was to make sure that it was a car the public could buy, not some one-time, zillion-dollar wonder. When the deadline came, Shelby had built only 12 of the cars. What could he do?

"We just painted blue stripes on the unfinished 88," recalls a Shelby man. "Then we parked them out by the 12 running cars. The racing officials never knew the difference."

Although you might not admire what Shelby did to get the G.T. 350 on the sales track, you'll admire what it did on the racetrack. The new super-Mustang was soon running wheel to wheel with Corvettes. Though the G.T. 350 wasn't as comfortable or as high-

To make the G.T. 350, Shelby started with a Mustang. He lightened it, tightened it and tuned it until it breathed fire.

tech as the 'Vette, it was just as fast and exciting! Today, Shelby-Mustangs are among the most valuable of classic Mustangs. A G.T. 350 in good condition is worth more than $100,000 to a collector—25 times what it sold for when new!

Most G.T. 350s were white with blue stripes. But there was a special model painted black with gold stripes. These Shelbys were called the G.T. 350H model, and were ordered by the Hertz Rent-A-Car company. Hertz knew the cars would be driven hard, but renters had to sign papers promising not to race them. Even so, more than one G.T. 350H was returned to its rental office covered

Shelby also built a more powerful version of the G.T. 350, with a big block 427-cubic-inch engine. It was called the G.T. 500.

with the marks left by number patches. Hertz quickly sold the cars. And they never even got to see the trophies their G.T. 350Hs must have won!

Over the years Shelby improved the G.T. 350, and he even came out with a bigger-engined, faster G.T. 500 model. The series came to an end by 1970, and each year only a few thousand were built. But the incredible Shelbys remain among the best-remembered Mustangs.

9 LONGER, LOWER AND HEAVIER

The first Mustang appeared in 1964. By 1967 more than a million and a half had been sold. The car was making money for Ford hand over fist.

One reason for the great sales was that there were no other cars like the Mustang. Ford knew this was too good to last. And as soon as the other carmakers saw what a hit the Mustang was, they raced to their drawing boards to get into the action.

Soon Detroit was full of rumors about new ponycars. GM was working on the Camaro, Chrysler was creating the Barracuda. Even American Motors was building a ponycar called the Javelin. And Ford Motor Company itself would soon add a second sports model. It was to be called the Cougar (the name designers wanted for the Mustang) and be sold through Mercury dealers.

The first new ponycar models were on sale by 1967, and they gave Mustang a real run for the money. Ford had to do something to keep the 'Stang in the lead.

Ford decided to fight off the competition by making the Mustang longer, lower, wider and much more powerful. Beginning with the

To fend off competition, Ford added this fastback
model soon after the original coupe and convertible
were introduced.

'67 model, the Mustang became a **musclecar**.

The first step was bolting in Ford's monster 390-cubic-inch, big
car V-8 engine. This power plant was usually used in the giant
LTD sedan. It had plenty of power—even more power than the G.T.
350. But it made the Mustang nose-heavy. The new pony was
lightning off the line, but didn't handle turns well.

When the Camaro and other competitors finally hit the showrooms, the drop in Mustang sales was greater than Ford ever
expected. The 1967 Mustang sold *127,000 fewer cars* than the year
before. Ouch!

This 1967 model is bigger and wider than the first Mustang design. Compare the size of the grille against earlier models.

In an effort to fight back Ford decided to go for new styling and even more power for the 1969 model. To get that power, the 390 V-8 made way for an even bigger engine, the Cobra-Jet 428.

Nowadays, three-liter engines are considered powerful, and the largest V-8s are about five liters in size. The Cobra-Jet was a full *seven* liters in size. The same engine was used in Ford's 200-mph Le Mans racing cars, though the racing version was more highly tuned.

Armed with the Cobra-Jet engine, the Mustang was a true roadburner. It could accelerate from zero to 60 mph in just over five seconds. But the car was more nose-heavy than ever. Even so, in 1971 Ford came out with an even bigger engine, the *Super*

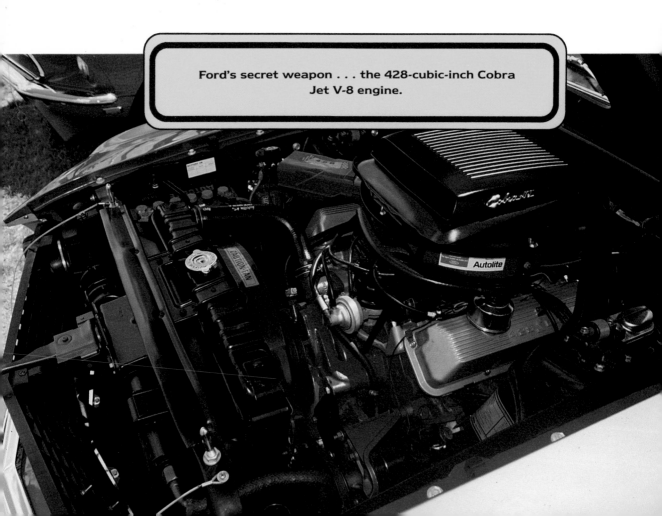

Ford's secret weapon . . . the 428-cubic-inch Cobra Jet V-8 engine.

Cobra Jet 429. Though only a cubic inch bigger in size, the new engine pumped a staggering 375 horsepower. All this in a car put together with Falcon parts!

Bigger engines meant a bigger car. By 1971 the once sleek Mustang had gained a half foot in length and almost 600 pounds in weight! It had also gained a thousand dollars in price. "What had once been a sleek horse was now more like a fat pig," Lee Iacocca said later.

Sales were in a slump. The magic name that caused riots in the streets and sold half a million cars a year now had trouble getting half that many out of the showroom. Barely six years after it was born, America's first ponycar seemed to be dying.

 **HERE COMES THE BOSS!**

Even in these dark moments, there were flashes of light. One of these was a model called the Boss 302.

In the late 1960s racing officials decided to create a new racing series around the ponycars. They thought that fans would be thrilled to see Mustangs, Camaros, Firebirds and 'Cudas take on each other. The new races would be known as "Trans-Am" Series. Each car company was invited to build a special model of its ponycar for the races. What incredible cars they were! There was the Camaro Z-28 and the Firebird Trans-Am, both still built today. Chrysler built the AAR (American Auto Racing) 'Cuda. Even American Motors raced their ponycar, the Javelin.

Ford knew the Cobra-Jet Mustang had the power to win Trans-Am races, but it was a poor handler. Besides, racing rules said that no engine could be bigger than 302 cubic inches. There was only one thing to do: enlarge the Mustang's original engine, the 289 V-8, to the largest legal size and take it racing. The new car became known as the "Boss 302."

Racing turned into winning. Ford won the first Trans-Am championship. And before long Ford put a street version of the Boss 302 on sale at its more than 8,000 showrooms.

What made the Boss great was that it was lightweight but still had power. Handling was well balanced. And if you worked the shift lever just right to keep engine speed up, you had a Mustang that was a real sports car.

Later, Ford built larger-engined "Boss" models called the Boss 351 and even a Boss 429, but most Mustang fans remember the 302 as the best of the breed.

Many Mustang fans consider the "Boss" series the best of the breed. Most prefer the small engine Boss 302 to this Boss 429.

11 THE INCREDIBLE SHRINKING MUSTANG

Although the Boss series cars won points in Mustang's favor, the drop in sales didn't stop.

Lee Iacocca had by now moved to a higher job at Ford, but he still had a special place for Mustang in his heart. And he kept on top of its problems.

Then one day, Lee and his designers had a brainstorm. If a bigger Mustang wasn't the answer, why not make it smaller?

At first the idea seemed crazy. Nobody in Detroit ever made a car smaller. You made it larger and more powerful. You gave the buyers more, and charged more for it.

But Iacocca knew Mustang buyers. They were young. Many were women who were turned off by the "macho man" Cobra-Jets. And because they'd just begun their careers, many Mustang buyers didn't have much money. The big-engine machines were expensive to buy, run and insure.

Suddenly Iacocca realized what had happened to the Mustang's success. "Our buyers didn't give up on us," he said. "We gave up on our buyers. We forgot what the original Mustang was all about." He ordered his best people to come up with a smaller Mustang for the 1974 model year.

Luckily Ford had recently set up ties with an Italian design company. On a hunch that company had created a small, four-cylinder Mustang dream car. When Iacocca heard about it, he put his team on the first plane to Italy. The Ford men saw the car and were thrilled with it. Within two months the model was at Ford headquarters, getting ready for production.

By 1969 the Mustang had turned into a bare-knuckled bruiser. Power was high, but sales were low.

The first Mustang was based on the Falcon, and the new car was also based on a sedan—Ford's new little Pinto. It used the Pinto's four-cylinder engine, as well as other Pinto parts. So Iacocca again created a new car at a bargain price.

Luck was with Iacocca in another way too. The new Mustang II, as it was called, was planned in the early 1970s when gas was cheap and easy to get. But in 1973 Arab nations turned off America's oil supply. Suddenly "No Gas" signs appeared at stations across the country. The few stations with any fuel to sell had long waiting lines. And when you could fill up, the price was unbelievably high. A gallon cost up to three times what it did before this "gas crisis." Suddenly everyone wanted gas-sippers, not gas-guzzlers. And if they could get one that was sporty and cheap, that was even better.

The new "mini-Mustang" sold 368,000 in its first year, almost as many sales as the first Mustang. Lightning may never strike twice, but success does...when you're Lee Iacocca.

Gas supplies returned to normal within a year, and people were getting used to the higher prices. Big cars were selling strongly again. But Ford had spent heavily to put the new baby Mustang on the market, and on the market it would stay.

By this time car magazines had tested the new pint-sized pony, and had found it lacking in punch. In the old days Ford would just install a V-8 and have all the go-power anyone wanted. But there was no room under the tiny hood for a V-8. A V-6 was the largest engine that would fit, and that didn't have the power Mustang drivers were used to.

Iacocca had remembered that Mustang customers like sporty looks and low prices, but he'd forgotten that they also liked some power. The sales of Mustang II dropped like a rock. Once again Ford's proud pony seemed headed for the final roundup.

Things were getting bad. Then they got worse. After 32 years with Ford Lee Iacocca was suddenly fired. He'd had problems getting along with big boss Henry Ford, and one day Henry called him in and said, "We think it's best if you leave the company."

A stunned Lee asked why.

"Sometimes you just don't like somebody," said Henry. Gee, Lee Iacocca thought later, it sure took him long enough to find that out! Mr. Ford never explained any further.

Iacocca became head of Chrysler—where he faced even bigger problems—the company was going broke! The Mustang remained at Ford, without the help of the man who created it. And it remained in deep trouble.

 **PLAY IT BACK, JACK!**

As the 1980s approached, Ford tried almost everything to regain the lost glory of its ponycar. They tried making it bigger and then smaller. It had been both a musclecar and an economy car. It was clear, nothing worked for long.

Within Ford a growing number of designers and engineers began thinking that the answer was simple: Build a normal-sized and -powered sporty car, make it as modern-looking as possible, and sell it at a fair price. After all, wasn't that what the first Mustang really was?

One man who felt this way was Jack Telnack. As a young designer, Telnack had worked on the original Mustang. Well, he sort of worked on it. He designed the wheel covers!

Now, though, Telnack was Ford's top designer. And he would have a big say in what the next Mustang would be like. The first

The 1972 Mustang was among the last of the "bigger is better" cars. In 1973 Ford switched to the "small is beautiful" four-cylinder Mustang II.

decision was easy. Junk the tiny Mustang II! The new car would be the same size as the wondrous '64—the car that started it all.

Next Telnack wanted a truly modern **chassis**. Luck was with him. The car still had to depend on sedan parts, but Ford had just built a very modern sedan called the Fairmont. Fairmont parts would go into the new 'Stang.

The engine choice was easy too. With a normal-sized body, a V-8 would again fit under the Mustang hood. But this would not be a nose-heavy monster like the Cobra-Jet. Instead, the new model would carry an improved 302 V-8. This classic engine had been used in earlier Mustangs. But now it had high-tech **fuel injection** and electronic engine controls, which gave the car both power and economy. Those who wanted more of a gas saver and a lower price could choose a four-cylinder engine or a V-6 in place of the V-8.

And finally the looks. They were always the most important part of any Mustang.

Before taking over Ford's design department, Telnack had worked in Ford factories overseas and had seen European designs. Cars in Europe were sleek and streamlined, as if they were shaped by the wind.

Telnack returned to Detroit when the new Mustang was about half-finished. He was anxious to see it, but when he did, he didn't like what he saw. Like other Ford cars of the seventies, the Mustang was boxy and old-fashioned.

"I sat down with the designers," Telnack says. "And I asked them to show me what *they* thought the car should look like. This wasn't the way things were done back then. You waited for your boss to tell you what he thought the car should be like, then you drew it. But in time, they realized I was serious."

When the designers let their ideas out, they were close to Telnack's. The team agreed that the new car should be extremely streamlined. It should not look like any former Mustang models or any other Ford car. It should just look good.

The car they created, the 1979 Mustang, was a winner! Lean and shapely, it featured a swept-back nose and a neatly rounded rear. Its sides were flat and clean, with no unnecessary bumps or vents. This design was the beginning of the rounded, streamlined "Ford look," later seen in the Thunderbird and in the wildly successful Taurus.

Designer Jack Telnack used European ideas on the all-new Mustang. The car was a hit! This pretty convertible is a 1986 GT model.

To Telnack, the '79 Mustang was the turning point. "Without the honesty we got in the Mustang," he says, "we'd never have those other cars today."

Sales picked right up. Mustang buyers liked what they saw and bought it. The design was so clean and attractive that for years it only needed minor changes to look fresh and new. It continues to look fresh and new today.

 **SVOs AND GTs**

After straining to energize the underpowered Mustang II, Ford engineers saw the return of the V-8 as a breath of fresh air. They also welcomed the chance to try out new ideas in tire and chassis design that would have been wasted on a smaller car.

One result was the Mustang TRX. This car was built around a new tire designed by Michelin of France. It was a hot road-handler.

Another new model was the Mustang SVO, named after Special Vehicle Operations—Ford's racing department. The SVO was high-performance all the way. Although the engine only had four cylinders, it was turbocharged for extra power. And special suspension parts, wheels and tires got that power to the road.

The SVO also featured fresh ideas in body design. Created to work with the wind at high speed, the car had special streamlining. Part of this "aero" system was a double wing by the rear window. That makes an SVO easy to spot from far away.

The most popular high-performance ponycar, however, has always been the Mustang GT, starring Ford's wonderful 302 engine. There's nothing fancy about the car. But since many of today's cars are more complex and costly than ever, that's a plus. The GT is one of the few cars a backyard mechanic can still tinker with, without first learning "turbo-talk and computerese."

Even without technical tricks the GT is a true high-performance car. It can jump from zero to 60 mph in just over six seconds and speed tops out at almost 140 mph. You can match that in a Porsche or Corvette, but it will cost three to four times the Mustang to do it.

Low cost and high performance have attracted a new kind of Mustang customer—the state police!

For years troopers have complained that their big, clumsy four-doors couldn't keep up with today's road rockets. So Ford built a cruiser version of the Mustang, complete with flashing light bar, gun rack and radar speedmeter. The police departments like it, and the troopers like it even more! Says one Connecticut trooper, "Tooling around in my little pony eight hours a day isn't a bad way to make a living."

The light but powerful 302-cubic-inch V-8 has long been a favorite of Mustang fans.

14 THE FUTURE OF THE MUSTANG

Although the Mustang has had to be reborn twice, it seems it will live forever! Ford has finally found the formula that works: Keep it lightweight, simple, modern-looking, fast and cheap. This combination has made the car a classic.

Of course, there will still be mistakes. A few years back Ford decided to build a new sporty car with Mazda, a Japanese firm. Each company had its own version of the car, but they shared many parts, including front-wheel drive and a Japanese-built engine. Mazda called its version the MX-6. Ford decided that their version would be the next Mustang.

When word leaked to the car magazines that the new Mustang was part Mazda, fans were outraged! Mail poured into Ford headquarters, protesting the coming "Maz-tang."

The Japanese build great machinery, but the fans felt that Mustang should be an all-American car. No Mazda motor! No Mazda anything! That was fine for other Ford cars, but not the Mustang.

Ford quickly changed its plan. The half-Japanese car was introduced, but it was called the "Probe," and sold well under that name. The all-American-built Mustang continued to sell.

Sometime soon—perhaps by the time you read this—there will be a new, all-American Mustang. It will keep the V-8 engine and **solid axle**, rear-wheel drive it's had since 1964. The looks will be new, but completely Mustang. Jack Telnack will see to that!

To be sure they will be giving fans what they want, Ford recently ran an unusual contest. Mustang lovers were asked to send in designs for the next Mustang. Then other fans were asked to vote for their favorite from among six choices. The contest winner gets a Mustang, of course!

The entries included some pretty wild sets of wheels. Some were shorter versions of the Thunderbird frame. Others used an all-new chassis. All of the engines had **overhead cam systems, multivalve** designs. Some had up to 32 valves, twice as many as the current 16, and some were made of lightweight aluminum. Transmissions had up to six speeds.

The body-style was low, wide and modern. Yet every design had parts of Mustang's long and glorious heritage. You could see hints

Mustangers are customizers. This ASC McLaren version adds aero streamlining and special wheels to an already pretty package.

of Telnack's wind-shaped lines. There was the look of power and speed of the Boss 302 and other Mustang musclecars. And there was the long hood and short rear gracefulness that first caught Lee Iacocca's eye almost 30 years before.

The new Mustang might look like one of these contest designs. Or it might not. But it will look good! And the price will stay low so that young people can afford to buy one.

The Mustang: It's one Cool Classic that keeps on getting better and better!

GLOSSARY/INDEX

chassis 38, 42   The underparts of a car.

clay models 12, 13   Designers create the shape of a new car in clay before metal is used. Clay can easily be reshaped to improve the looks. The clay may be painted to look like metal.

designer 12, 13, 39   Creator of a car's appearance and general layout.

engineer 8, 37   The person who sets out how the car's engine systems and other parts will work.

fastback 19   A term designers use for a streamlined auto body style. The roof flows in a single curve all the way to the rear of the car, without the usual trunk shape. Luggage is often put into the car through an opening in the roof called a hatchback. Cars with the usual separate trunk shape are called "notchbacks."

fuel injection 39   A system that actively pumps the fuel-air mixture into an engine rather than having it drift in. Replaces the carburetor.

multivalve engine 45   An engine with more than the usual one intake and one exhaust valve per cylinder. The more valve openings in a cylinder, the easier for gas to enter and exhaust to leave, making the engine run with more power.

musclecar 27, 44   A small car with a very large engine. Popular in the 1960s. The first musclecar was the 1963 Pontiac GTO.

mustang 17   A wild horse of the American west. The Ford Mustang features a sculpture of this horse on its nameplate.

overhead cam system 45   A way of opening engine valves that puts the opening parts right over the valves. Eliminates former use of long pushrods running down into the engine.

solid axle 44   A way of mounting rear wheels on a single beam. Low in cost to produce, but can cause both wheels to bounce when one hits a bump.